MW01282438

# THE WISDOM OF

# MARCUS

# AURELIUS

### Translated by ROBIN WATERFIELD

BASIC BOOKS

New York

Copyright © 2025 by Robin Waterfield

Cover design by Chin-Yee Lai
Cover images © G. Dagli Orti/© NPL-DEA Picture Library/Bridgeman
Images; © Detchana Wangkheeree/Shutterstock.com
Cover copyright © 2025 by Hachette Book Group, Inc.

Hachette Book Group supports the right to free expression and the value of
copyright. The purpose of copyright is to encourage writers and artists to
produce the creative works that enrich our culture.

The scanning, uploading, and distribution of this book without permission is
a theft of the author's intellectual property. If you would like permission to
use material from the book (other than for review purposes), please contact
permissions@hbgusa.com. Thank you for your support of the author's rights.

Basic Books
Hachette Book Group
1290 Avenue of the Americas, New York, NY 10104
www.basicbooks.com

Printed in the United States of America

Originally published in unabridged hardcover by Basic Books in April 2021
First Abridged Hardcover Edition: March 2025

Published by Basic Books, an imprint of Hachette Book Group, Inc. The Basic
Books name and logo is a registered trademark of the Hachette Book Group.

The Hachette Speakers Bureau provides a wide range of authors for speaking
events. To find out more, go to hachettespeakersbureau.com or email
HachetteSpeakers@hbgusa.com.

Basic Books may be purchased in bulk for business, educational, or
promotional use. For more information, please contact your local
bookseller or the Hachette Book Group Special Markets Department
at special.markets@hbgusa.com.

The publisher is not responsible for websites (or their content) that are not
owned by the publisher.

Print book interior design by Bart Dawson.

Library of Congress Cataloging-in-Publication Data

Names: Marcus Aurelius, Emperor of Rome, 121–180, author. | Waterfield,
    Robin, 1952– translator.
Title: The wisdom of Marcus Aurelius / translated by Robin Waterfield.
Other titles: Meditations. Selections (Waterfield). English
Description: First abridged hardcover edition. | New York : Basic Books, 2025. |
Identifiers: LCCN 2024029836 | ISBN 9781541606760 (abridged hardcover) |
    ISBN 9781541606784 (abridged ebook)
Subjects: LCSH: Marcus Aurelius, Emperor of Rome, 121–180. | Ethics–Early
    works to 1800. | Stoics–Early works to 1800. | Life–Early works to 1800.
Classification: LCC B581 .W38 2025 | DDC 188–dc23/eng/20241125
LC record available at https://lccn.loc.gov/2024029836

ISBNs: 9781541673854 (hardcover), 9781541675605 (ebook),
9781541673861 (paperback), 9781541606760 (abridged hardcover),
9781541606784 (abridged ebook)

LSC-C

Printing 1, 2024

# CONTENTS

# INTRODUCTION

Marcus Aurelius Antoninus, to give him his short imperial name, was the sixteenth emperor of Rome, from March 7, 161, until his death at the age of fifty-eight on March 17, 180. Marcus is regarded as the last in a series of five good emperors, but he himself tried to model his character and behavior, as emperor, on that of his immediate predecessor, Antoninus Pius (reigned 138–161), whom he regarded as a perfect exemplar.

Marcus did his best to put his philosophical principles to work in his edicts and behavior, but his reign was troubled. For almost all of it the Antonine Plague raged. This pandemic cannot be securely identified, but by the time it died out toward the end of the century, it had killed many millions. Marcus's brother and co-emperor, Lucius Verus, was one of the victims, leaving Marcus as sole emperor from January 169 onward. Then again, border wars and sometimes insurrections within the empire were an emperor's almost inevitable lot, and Marcus was no exception. In fact, he died while campaigning on the Danube against Germanic peoples who were aiming to encroach on Roman territory. He died not as a result of wounds—he probably never actually fought—but of general ill health. He had suffered throughout his life from tuberculosis and its concomitant ailments.

During the years of this campaign in Central Europe Marcus had been writing a kind of journal. Miraculously, the twelve notebooks, with their 490 or so handwritten entries, that constitute this journal were found after his death and preserved. Although not intended by Marcus for publication, some centuries later the journal did finally gain public recognition, and since then it has been perhaps the best-known and best-loved work of inspirational popular philosophy in the Western world. We call the book simply Marcus Aurelius's *Meditations*.

It is astonishing that the wealthiest and most powerful man in Europe—in the world, as far as he knew—was modest and self-critical enough to have written such a book. Marcus constantly restores one's faith in human nature. The book's popularity rests on its accessibility. Marcus treats himself as an ordinary person, not as the absolute ruler of fifty million souls. The book is deeply personal—the "you" whom Marcus frequently addresses is always himself—but we recognize ourselves in what Marcus says about himself because we share his flaws and aspirations, and therefore respond to his admonishments and advice.

Marcus's philosophical framework was Stoicism. He was attracted to Stoicism in part because the school allowed or even encouraged would-be philosophers to play a public role, whereas the other main philosophical school, Epicureanism, counseled withdrawal from the world as the only way to attain peace of mind. Such retirement was not a possibility for the emperor of Rome, and throughout *Meditations* Marcus expresses his distaste for this and other aspects of Epicureanism. Contrary to Epicureanism, the Stoics believed that peace of mind can come from engaging with the world in the right way, and especially from recognizing that all the thoughts and feelings that disrupt tranquility are generated by one's own mind, and can therefore be dispelled by one's own mind.

As emperor, however—and as Marcus sometimes complains—he had little or no time for study, no time to continue the theoretical work that would have occupied some of his time in his youth. But there was more to Stoicism than theory. In the ancient world the philosophical schools filled a major gap that religion, which was based solidly on ritual practice, could not cover. That is, if you wanted to become a morally better person, and even to aspire to enlightenment (to become a sage, as the Stoics put it), you practiced philosophy. The new salvationist religion of Christianity was on the rise during Marcus's reign, but the old pagan ways still prevailed. It was this ethical, character-changing aspect of Stoicism that Marcus sought to practice. It required a thorough and ongoing overhaul of his set of beliefs and a thorough reset of his goals in life. It required him not to trust his feelings and emotions, his hopes and fears, but to rely only on reason in order to align himself with the divine, benevolently providential Reason that steers the universe and every part of it, however small. Throughout *Meditations* we see Marcus struggling to get all this right, and as readers we internalize his struggle.

The great majority of the journal entries, then, are, above all, Marcus's way of "dyeing his mind" (as he puts it at one point) with the ideas and teachings that could help him be a better person and a better emperor. The entries are fragments of a kind of dialogue between teacher and pupil, where Marcus simultaneously plays both parts. For Marcus, the notebooks and their entries had a therapeutic aim: to reinforce and revive, if necessary, the moral precepts he had come to accept as true, as a way of helping him put them into practice. Each entry is, as it were, a dose of therapeutic medicine as well as a reminder of how he should be acting.

While knowing about Stoicism helps readers appreciate where Marcus is coming from, no such knowledge is required to profit from the book, because Marcus addresses general life issues that strike chords with everyone. Marcus's struggle, though framed in Stoic terms, is the same struggle that is experienced by anyone who is determined to keep themselves squarely on the path of self-improvement. Stoic practice was for Marcus the cure for the disease of attachment to worldly and material things, for the nightmare of being "tugged here and there" by impulses and random thoughts and feelings. He understood that if you don't know what's moving you at any instant, you are not in control of your life.

———

The extracts that make up this little book are drawn from my translation of the complete work: *Marcus Aurelius, Meditations: The Annotated Edition* (Basic Books, 2021). In a few cases—for the purposes of this version, and for the sake of improvement—I have tweaked the original translation.

Certain themes are dominant in the notebooks. First, Marcus had a poor constitution and thought a lot about death. Second, as emperor, every day Marcus had to consult with his advisers, receive petitions, dictate letters, and so on; but he frequently confides unguarded thoughts to his journal about how irritating and even offensive he found at least some of the people he had to deal with. Third, he reflects a lot on posthumous fame. This might seem a trivial subject for him to have focused on, but he was the emperor of Rome, and his deeds were bound to be noted, and later recorded by historians. We can think of it for ourselves, though we are not emperors, as wanting recognition or the respect of others.

Naturally, then, these three topics feature in this pocket-sized *Meditations*. But I have also selected Marcus's take on a wide range of topics that are likely to be of personal interest to twenty-first-century readers—or indeed to readers of any generation. There are gaps: Marcus has little or nothing to say, for instance, about war and peace, or about love, friendship, and sex. But he has plenty of wise, thought-provoking, and sometimes surprising ideas about many other aspects of the world and human life. I hope this little book will attract new readers to Marcus's work, and I hope that those who already know and appreciate the longer edition will find this one handy for their pockets, purses, and rucksacks.

# THE WISDOM OF
# MARCUS
# AURELIUS

# — ON —
# AIMS AND ENDS

---

In all you do, be a disciple of Antoninus: his ener-getic approach to rational action, his constant equability, his piety, the composure of his features, his kindness, his lack of vain self-importance, and his determination to get to the heart of mat-ters. Then there was the way he'd refuse to let anything go until thorough examination had led him to understand it perfectly; how he put up with unfair criticism without being critical in return; how he never rushed things; and how he refused to listen to malicious gossip. He was an accurate judge of character and what people did, without being disparaging, timid, distrustful, or sophistic. He was easily satisfied when it came to things like lodgings, bedding, clothes, food, and attendants. He was industrious, patient, and able to stay in place until evening because, thanks to his frugal diet, he didn't need to evacuate waste except at his habitual time. He was a reliable and consistent friend. He was tolerant of frank criticism of his plans and happy if someone could show him a better way. He was religious without being superstitious. If in all these respects you're his disciple, the hour of your death will find you with as clear a conscience as his.

———

No more abstract discussions about what a good man is like: just be one!

———

If you ever get to call yourself good, moral, honest, conscientious, amenable, and dignified, never exchange these labels for others or lose them. And, if you do lose them, recover them quickly. If you consistently deserve these labels (without longing to hear them applied to you by others), you'll be a changed man and you'll enter upon a changed life. To remain as you've been up to now, to be mangled and defiled in the kind of life you live at present, is an extremely stupid form of clinging to life. If you find yourself backsliding and losing control, don't despair, but secrete yourself in a corner where you can recover control.

You must always consider how to tackle any matter that arises with scrupulous and unfeigned grace, affection for others, generosity, and justice, and how to spend no time over any other incoming impressions. That will happen if you treat every act as though it were the last of your life—which is to say, if you're free from all stray thoughts and from any deviation, under the influence of emotion, from the principles established by reason, and if you're free from hypocrisy, self-love, and dissatisfaction with your lot. And look! There are only a few things that a person has to master in order to gain the ability to live a contented and god-fearing life. Even the gods will require nothing more from someone who adheres to these few principles.

If you carry out every present task by following right reason assiduously, resolutely, and with kindness; if, rather than getting distracted by irrelevancies, you keep your guardian spirit unspoiled and steady, as though you had to surrender it at any moment; if you engage with the task not with expectations or evasions, but satisfied if your current performance is in accord with nature; and if what you say and express is spoken with true Roman honesty, you'll be living the good life. And there's no one who can stop you doing so!

Don't stray, but do what's right whenever you're moved to act, and stick with what's clear and certain whenever you think.

# — ON —
# ANGER
# MANAGEMENT

---

Remember also how many people spent their lives seeing others as their enemies, suspecting them, hating them, battling with them, only to be laid out for burial and burned to ashes—and put an end to your resentment.

---

We suffer more from getting angry and upset about such things than we do from the things themselves which are making us angry and upset.

―――――

Surely you're not angry with a man because of his foul stench or stinking breath, are you? What good will that do you? That's the way his mouth is, that's the way his armpits are, so they're bound to give off foul odors. "But, as a human being, he's been equipped with the faculty of reason, and has the ability, if he applies his mind, to realize what's making him so offensive." Fine, but it follows that you have the faculty of reason too. Use rationality to activate rationality: explain things to him, bring the matter up with him. If he gets the point, you'll cure him and there'll be no need for anger.

―――――

When you're too angry or impatient, remember that human life is fleeting and before long all of us will have been laid to rest.

---

How cruel it is to thwart people's attempts to get what they think is proper to them and expedient for them! And yet, in a sense, you act as just such an obstacle when you get cross with them for their flaws. I mean, they're bound in any case to be drawn to what they take to be proper to them and to their advantage. "But they're wrong!" So instruct them and explain things to them, without getting angry.

---

It's not just getting angry with people that you should avoid, but flattering them as well. Neither flattery nor anger contribute to the common good and both have harmful consequences. Every time you lose your temper, make sure you have readily available the thought that anger is not a manly quality, and that in fact gentleness and calmness are more manly, qua more human.

_____

It won't make any difference: they won't stop even if you explode with rage.

_____

It's pointless to let mere *things* make you angry, since they lack the ability to care.

———

The moment you find yourself offended by a flaw in someone, you should stop and consider whether you have similar flaws. Are you, for instance, taking money to be a good thing, or pleasure, or fame, or anything of that kind? This idea will quickly make you forget your anger, because you'll realize that he had no choice in the matter. I mean, what's he to do? If you can, however, you should get rid of whatever it is that's leaving him no choice.

———

The gods, who are immortal, don't resent the fact that for all eternity they'll inevitably and always be obliged to tolerate so many despicable creatures. In fact, they even take care of them in all sorts of ways. So won't you, who have only the shortest time to live, renounce resentment, especially since you're one of the despicable creatures?

———

People with jaundice find honey bitter, those who've been bitten by a rabid dog have an aversion to water, and to little boys a ball is something to admire. So why am I angry? Do you think that false opinions have less influence than bile does on jaundice and poison on hydrophobics?

———

# — ON —
# BEAUTY

So then, anything that's fine, in any sense of the word, owes this to itself and is complete in itself, and praise forms no part of it. At any rate, praise has no effect for better or worse on anything that's fine, and I mean this to apply also to entities that are commonly called fine in the sense of beautiful, such as material objects or works of art. So does what is truly fine need anything apart from itself? No more than law does, or truth, or benevolence, or modesty. Is the fineness of any of these things preserved by its being praised, or destroyed by its being disparaged? Does an emerald's beauty fade if it isn't praised? And what about gold, ivory, purple, a lyre, a knife, a flower, a bush?

———————

So there's almost nothing that a sensitive person, with a deep enough understanding of the workings of the universe, will fail to find pleasing in its manifestations, including these incidental concomitants. He gets as much pleasure from seeing the gaping jaws of actual wild beasts as he does from the secondhand representations of them by painters and sculptors. He's able to see a kind of perfection and beauty in the elderly of both sexes, and to view the sexual attractiveness of his slaves with chaste eyes. And although most people will find few such cases plausible, that's because they are not genuinely familiar with nature and its works.

———————

# — ON —
# BELIEF

---

In themselves, the things of the world have no effect on the mind; they can't get through to it, they can't sway it, and they can't stir it. The only thing that changes and stirs the mind is the mind.

---

Today I freed myself from all the things that were afflicting me, or it would be more accurate to say that I *ejected* all the things that were afflicting me, because they weren't outside me, but inside, inherent in my beliefs.

———

Remember that "Everything is as you take it to be"—and that what you take things to be is up to you. Anytime you want to, then, you can eliminate the belief and, like a sailor after rounding a headland, you'll find calm water, perfect stillness, and an unruffled bay.

———

———

What's detrimental to you doesn't depend on someone else's command center, and certainly not on some worsening or alteration of surrounding conditions. On what, then? On that part of you that takes things to be bad. If it believes no such thing, all is well. Even if what is closest to it, the body, undergoes surgery or cautery, or is left to suppurate or putrefy, you should still get the part of you that forms beliefs to keep quiet—that is, to judge that nothing that can happen equally to bad and good people is either bad or good. After all, anything that happens equally to people whether their lives are dissonant or consonant with nature is itself neither consonant nor dissonant with nature.

———

# — ON —
# BLAMING OTHERS

There's no point in assigning blame, because either you can set the person straight, in which case you should do that, or, if you can't do that, you should straighten out the business itself. And if you can't do that, what's to be gained by assigning blame? There's no point in doing something pointless.

The gods are not to be blamed, because they do no wrong, either deliberately or involuntarily. Nor are men to be blamed, because they do no wrong that isn't involuntary. So don't blame anyone.

---

Whenever a person's lack of shame offends you, you should immediately ask yourself: "So is it possible for there to be no shameless people in the world?" It isn't, and you should therefore stop demanding the impossible. He's just one of those shameless people who must necessarily exist in the world. You should keep the same thought readily available also for when you're faced with devious and untrustworthy people, and people who are flawed in any way. As soon as you remind yourself that it's impossible for such people not to exist, you'll be kinder toward each and every one of them.

---

————

Besides, have you been harmed in any way? You'll find that none of the people who make you lose your temper has done anything that might affect your mind for the worse; and outside of the mind there's nothing that is truly detrimental or harmful for you. Moreover, what is unusual or surprising about an uneducated man doing uneducated things? It's worth considering whether you ought rather to blame yourself for failing to foresee that he would transgress in this way. But, above all, when you find fault with someone for lack of fidelity or gratitude, turn and look at yourself, because the fault was plainly yours. In the first instance, your mistake was to have trusted a man with such a character not to let you down; in the second, you failed to do the favor for its own sake, on the assumption that you would immediately reap your full reward just from the action itself.

————

If you treat things that aren't subject to your volition as good or bad, it's inevitable that, when you meet one of these "bad" things or fail to gain one of these "good" things, you'll blame the gods and hate the people who are responsible for what happened, or who you suspect may be responsible for such a thing in the future. In fact, many of the wrongs we commit are a consequence of our assigning value to these things. But if we judge only things that are up to us to be good and bad, you'll be left with no reason to criticize the gods or adopt a hostile attitude toward other people.

# — ON —
# THE BODY

———

There are three things of which you are com-posed: body, spirit, mind. Of these, the first two belong to you insofar as it's your job to care for them, but, properly speaking, only the third is really yours. It follows that if you separate from yourself—that is, from your mind—all that other people do or say, all that you yourself have done or said, all that disturbs your peace of mind as looming in the future, all the properties of the body that encases you or of the spirit that is embedded in it that are not subject to your volition, and all that swirls around you, driven by the whirlwind of the external world, until your mind has been released from the bonds of fate, and lives purified, untrammeled, on its own, doing what is right, willingly accepting everything that happens, and speaking the truth—if, I say, you detach your command center from what has become attached to it as a result of its being attracted by bodily feelings, and from all that is to come and all that has gone, and make yourself, in Empedocles's words, "a rounded sphere, rejoicing in encircling solitude," and train yourself to live the only life you have, that is in the present moment, you'll be able to pass what remains of your life, up until your death, with a mind that is tranquil in itself, kind to others, and at peace with your guardian spirit.

---

———

The body should be firm and not ungainly, whether it's in motion or at rest. The kinds of provisions the mind makes for the face in order to maintain an intelligent and decorous expression are also required for the body as a whole as well. But all this must be attended to in a matter-of-fact manner.

———

Visualize the freedom with which reason moves through everything—as fire moves up, as a stone moves down, as a roller rolls down a slope—and look no farther. For all other obstacles are either due to the body, worthless corpse that it is, or else they cause no damage or harm at all unless the mind believes it so or reason itself permits them to.

God sees all command centers stripped of their material vessels, their worthless casings, because he has only his intelligence with which to make contact, and the only contact he has is with what has flowed and been channeled from him to them. If you too get into the habit of doing likewise, you'll rid yourself of many distractions. After all, is it at all likely that a man who's blind to the flesh that encases him will waste his time admiring clothing, houses, or any such trappings and stage sets?

What is my command center to me? What am I making it at the moment? What am I currently using it for? Is it devoid of intelligence? Is it disengaged and cut off from society? Is it so attached to and implicated with the body that it's being moved by its movements?

You're a pathetic little soul sustaining a corpse, as Epictetus used to say.

# — ON —
# CAUSE AND
# EFFECT

---

In the universe at large everything is intercon-
nected, and just as all bodies together make up
the specific body that is the universe, so all causes
together make up the specific cause that is fate.

---

A man ejaculates into a womb and withdraws, and then another cause takes over and fashions a finished baby. What incredible causes! What an incredible result! Next, the child releases some food down its throat, and then another cause takes over and creates sensation, motivation— life, in short, and strength, and a whole lot of other incredible results. Think about these processes, which go on quite invisibly, and see the power behind them. It's the same kind of seeing that enables us to see the power that makes things fall or rise; in neither case do we use our eyes, but the powers are no less apparent for that.

There are two reasons, then, why you should gladly accept whatever happens to you. First, because the experience happened to you, was prescribed for you, and was the product of a web somehow woven just for you way back in time, out of the most ancient causes. Second, because, for the directing principle of the universe, even what happens to each of us as individuals plays a part in its advancement, perfection, and, by Zeus, its very preservation. After all, any whole is impaired if you cut the connection and continuity of its parts to any extent at all, and the same goes if you cut the chain of its causes. But this is what you do, insofar as it's in your power, whenever you're dissatisfied with your lot. In a sense, this is an act of destruction.

Remind yourself at frequent intervals how quickly things and events are carried past and swept away. Reality is like an endlessly flowing river, its activities constantly changing, its causes variable beyond counting.

---

What comes next is always related by affinity to what went before. It's not a matter of mere enumeration of discrete units in a mechanically inevitable sequence, but of a rational connection. Just as existing things are arrayed in harmonious relation to one another, so things in the process of coming into existence don't exhibit mere succession, but a wonderful affinity.

---

Whatever happens to you was being created for you from eternity, and from eternity the web of causation was weaving for you not just your existence, but this particular event as well.

# —— ON ——
# CHANGE

———

Remember that in a short while you won't exist at all, and the same goes for everything that you now see and all the people now alive. It's a fact of nature that everything changes, deteriorates, and perishes, so that the next generation of things can come into existence.

———

———

Everything is changing. You yourself are constantly changing and, in a sense, perishing, and so is the universe as a whole.

———

Is change something to fear? But can anything happen without change? Is there anything that's nearer and dearer to universal nature? What about you personally? Can you take a warm bath unless the firewood undergoes change? Can you be nourished unless your food undergoes change? Can anything else worthwhile take place without change? So don't you see that the changes that *you* experience are no different, and are similarly necessary to universal nature?

———

Green grape, ripe grape, dried grape: every phase a change, not into nonexistence, but simply into a state that didn't exist at the time.

In no time at all, everything you see will be changed by the nature that directs the universe. It will use their substance to create more things, and then it will use the substance of these things to create still more things, in order to keep the universe forever young.

Time is a river of events and its current is strong: no sooner does something heave into view than it's swept away and something else is being carried past instead, only to be swept away.

Whatever you encounter in life, consider its origin, what it's made of, what it's changing into, what it will be like after it's changed, and that it will come to no harm as a result of changing.

# — ON —
# CONTENTMENT
# AND JOY

---

Find your bliss in simplicity, modesty, and indifference to the whole range of things between virtue and vice. Love humankind. Follow God's lead.

---

"Do little," he says, "if you want to be content." But wouldn't it be better to do what's *necessary*—everything the reason of a naturally social being requires, and in the manner in which it requires it? The upshot will not only be the contentment that comes from doing the right thing, but also the contentment that comes from doing little. After all, most of our words and actions are unnecessary, and dispensing with them gives one more freedom and greater peace of mind. It follows that you should prod yourself every time by asking: Is this really necessary? And it's important to dispense not only with unnecessary actions, but unnecessary thoughts as well, because that will ensure that no redundant actions follow either.

Your life must be constructed one action at a time, and if each action is performed as successfully as may be, you can be content. And no one can prevent you from carrying them out successfully. "But something external will get in the way." Nothing, at any rate, that can stop you acting with justice, moderation, and sound judgment. "But I may be stopped from being effective in other ways." Yes, but by cheerfully accepting the obstacle itself and by turning, in a spirit of compromise, to what's feasible instead, another action takes the place of the hindered one, and will contribute to the construction of your life.

———

Find joy and rest in one thing alone: in moving from one socially useful act to another, while remaining mindful of God.

———

# — ON —
# COPING WITH
# OTHER PEOPLE

---

At the start of the day tell yourself: I shall meet people who are officious, ungrateful, abusive, treacherous, malicious, and selfish. In every case, they've got like this because of their ignorance of good and bad. But I have seen goodness and badness for what they are, and I know that what is good is what is morally right, and what is bad is what is morally wrong; and I've seen the true nature of the wrongdoer himself and know that he's related to me—not in the sense that we share blood and seed, but by virtue of the fact that we both partake of the same intelligence, and so of a portion of the divine. None of them can harm me, anyway, because none of them can infect me with immorality, nor can I become angry with someone who's related to me, or hate him, because we were born to work together, like feet or hands or eyelids, like the rows of upper and lower teeth. To work against each other is therefore unnatural—and anger and rejection count as "working against."

———

Only one thing is important: to behave throughout your life toward the liars and crooks around you with kindness, honesty, and justice.

———

If, while taking exercise, someone scratches us with his nails or butts us with his head as he breaks out of a hold, we don't blame him or take offense or suspect him subsequently of wishing us ill. True, we exercise caution and try to avoid being hurt again, but in a kindly fashion, not because we regard him as malicious or suspect him of anything. That's how we should behave in the rest of our lives as well. We should overlook much of what those whom we could call our wrestling partners do. After all, as I said, one may avoid trouble without being suspicious or hostile.

It's best to leave someone else's transgression there with him.

The best form of defense is not to become like one's enemy.

———

The vain pomp of a procession, plays on a stage, flocks, herds, skirmishes, a meager bone tossed to puppies, a scrap of bread tossed in a fish tank, the toiling of ants with their burdens, the scurrying of nervous mice, puppets tugged by their strings. In the midst of all this, you should take a stand good-naturedly and without being bigheaded, but paying attention to the fact that the worth of every individual depends on the worth of what he values.

———

Get into the habit of listening attentively to anything that anyone says, and enter, as much as you can, into the mind of the speaker.

---

The first question to ask yourself when you meet someone is "Where does he stand on goodness and badness?" For if he believes such-and-such about pleasure and pain and what gives rise to them, about fame and obscurity, and about death and life, I won't be surprised or taken aback if he acts in such-and-such a way, and I'll remember that he has no choice but to act in that way.

---

Don't waste what remains of your life thinking about other people, unless you do so with reference to the welfare of the state—I mean wondering what so-and-so is doing and why, or what he's saying, what he's thinking, what his designs are, and so on, which distracts you from paying attention to your own command center.

When you want to cheer yourself up, think of the positive qualities of your friends and acquaintances: the efficiency of one, for instance, the moral sensibility of another, the generosity of a third, and so on. Nothing is more cheering than when the virtues are manifest in the characters of your friends and acquaintances, and especially when they occur all at once, insofar as that is feasible. So you should keep them in the forefront of you mind.

Don't align your thinking with that of the man who's dishonoring you. Don't think as he wants you to think, but see things as they truly are.

———

Judge yourself entitled to say or do anything that's in accord with nature, and don't let yourself be talked out of it by any criticism or argument that may follow as a consequence. If it was the right thing to do or say, don't put yourself down. Other people have their own command centers and their own impulses, and you shouldn't let your attention be caught by them, but carry straight on, following your own nature and universal nature, two things that share a single path.

———

# — ON —
# DEATH

---

If a god informed you that you were going to die tomorrow, or the day after at the latest, you'd hardly think it mattered whether it was tomorrow or the day after, at any rate unless you were hopelessly small-minded. It's not as if there were much difference in time involved. By the same token, you should consider it an utterly trivial matter whether your life lasts for years or comes to an end tomorrow.

---

It's as though a praetor, after engaging an actor for a comedy, were to dismiss him mid-show. "But I haven't played all five acts, only three!" Quite so, but in life the play might be over after three acts. The ending is decided by the one who was formerly responsible for your constitution and is now responsible for your disintegration. You have no responsibility for either. Go serenely, then, matching the serenity of the god who is dismissing you.

———

Don't act as though you were going to live for ten thousand years. Fate is hanging over your head. While you live—while you can—be a good man.

———

Death brings relief from reacting to sense impressions, from being tugged here and there by one's impulses, from associative thinking, and from service to the body.

---

I make my way on nature's road until the time comes for me to fall and take my rest, sending my final breath into the air I daily breathe, and falling on the earth from which my father garnered his seed, my mother her blood, and my nurse her milk—the earth which has supplied my food and drink day after day for so many years—the earth which bears me as I trample it and abuse it in so many ways.

Alexander of Macedon and the man who tended his mules were made equal by death.

———

You embarked, set sail, and reached land. Step ashore. If it takes you to another life—well, nothing is devoid of gods, even there. If it takes you to a state of insensibility, you'll no longer have to endure pain and pleasure, and you'll no longer be in thrall to a bodily vessel which is as far inferior as that which is serving it is superior. For the latter is mind and guardian spirit, while the former is earth and blood.

———

An unphilosophical but still effective method for helping you to scorn death is to run over a list of people who clung tenaciously to life, asking yourself what they gained over those who died young. One way or another, they're all in their graves now. The span of one's life is altogether insignificant—and look at the experiences, the kinds of people, and the poor body one has to endure while seeing out the time! Don't regard your life as in any way important, then. Look behind you at the yawning gulf of time and see the other immeasurable stretch ahead. From this point of view, what's the difference between a baby who lives for three days and someone who lives three times as long as Nestor?

Don't belittle death, but welcome it as one of many expressions of nature's will. Disintegration is no different from any other natural process that life's seasons bring: youth and age; growth and maturity; teething, growing a beard, hair turning gray; conception, pregnancy, childbirth. So what's appropriate for someone who has thought things through isn't treating death as something to be dismissed or ignored or despised, but waiting for it on the understanding that it's a natural process.

No one is so fortunate that there won't be some people standing by his deathbed who welcome the "dire event." Suppose he was serious and wise: there'll be someone there at the end who'll say to himself: "What a relief to be rid of that stickler at last! Not that he was ever openly hard on us, but I could sense his tacit disapproval." That's what they'd say about such a man, but what about me? How many more reasons there are for being greatly relieved at being shot of me! When you come to die, then, you'll think of this and your departure will be eased by the realization that "The life I'm leaving is one in which even my associates, on whose behalf I labored, prayed, and brooded so much—even they want to see me gone, and are probably hoping that my death will make life easier for them." So why would anyone want to cling on to life and prolong his stay here?

Surely you don't resent the fact that you weigh only so many pounds and not three hundred? By the same token, there's no point in resenting the fact that you're going to live only so many years and not more. You're happy with the amount of substance that has been allocated to you, and by the same token you should be happy with the time allocated to you as well.

Think about what kind of person you must be, in body and soul, when overtaken by death.

# — ON —
# DEATH AS NOTHING TO FEAR

Nothing bad happens to any action at all that comes to an end at the appropriate time, just because it has come to an end, and nothing bad happens either to the person who performed the action, just because it has come to an end. By the same token, then, the totality of all actions, which is a life, suffers nothing bad, provided that it comes to a timely end, just because it has come to an end, and nothing bad happens either to the person who brings this sequence of actions to a timely end. The time and the cutoff point of a life are given by nature, sometimes by one's own nature, as when one dies of old age, but in general by universal nature, which by the changing of its parts keeps the whole universe forever young and fresh. Now, anything that benefits the universe is bound to be altogether fine and timely, and it therefore follows that the ending of life isn't bad for the individual (nor is it shameful, because it's not a matter that's subject to his volition and it doesn't have a negative effect on the common good), but actually good, because it's timely for the universe, benefits it, and is compatible with it.

———

———

To be afraid of death is to be afraid of either unconsciousness or a different kind of consciousness. But if death is the end of consciousness, you won't be conscious of anything bad either. And if you gain a different kind of consciousness, you'll be a different kind of creature, which is to say that you'll still be alive.

———

A man for whom only what is appropriate is good, to whom it is irrelevant whether the number of actions he carries out as dictated by right reason is greater or smaller, and to whom it makes no difference whether the time he has to see the world is longer or shorter—to such a man even death is nothing to fear.

———

Everything you do and say and think should be predicated on the possibility of your imminent departure from life. But, if the gods exist, leaving this world can't be something to fear, because they wouldn't let anything bad happen to you. On the other hand, if they don't exist or have no care for the human race, why live in such a world, devoid of gods and divine providence? But in fact they do exist and they do care for the human race, and they've made it entirely up to each of us to avoid experiencing anything truly bad. And if anything else were bad, they would also have made sure that it was our choice whether or not to experience that too. (But how could a man's life be made worse by anything that doesn't make him a worse person?) The universe would have neglected this only if it were ignorant, or if it had knowledge but lacked the ability to guard against it or correct it; but neither of these is the case. Nor could it have committed such a great wrong, out of either impotence or incompetence, as to let good and bad things be the lot equally of good and bad people without distinction. But death and life, glory and obscurity, pain and pleasure, wealth and poverty—all these things come to good and bad people alike, since they are morally neutral in themselves, and this proves that they're neither good nor bad.

———

It is for the intellectual faculty to consider what death is, and the fact that, if one sees it for what it is and, by analyzing the concept, dissolves the impressions that adhere to it, one will stop believing it to be anything other than a natural process—and there's nothing to fear about natural processes unless you're a child—though in fact not only is it a product of nature, but it also does nature good.

# — ON —
# DOING GOOD

---

If you've done someone good, what more do you want? Aren't you satisfied with having acted in conformity with your nature? Do you want remuneration as well? It's as if the eyes sought compensation for seeing or the feet for walking. Just as eyes and feet were made for a particular purpose, which fulfills them because the performance of that function is what they were designed to do, so, because human beings were made to do others good, when a man does something that benefits someone else, he's doing what he was made for, and is fulfilled.

---

One kind of person, when he does someone a good turn, is also ready to calculate the monetary value of the thanks owed to him. Another may not go so far, but he still privately thinks of the other person as in his debt and is conscious of what he's done. Yet another, however, is in a sense not even conscious of what he's done, but resembles a vine which, after bearing grapes, doesn't immediately go in search of something else to do, once it has borne the fruit that's proper to it. Or you could say he resembles a horse after a gallop, a hound after a hunt, a bee that has made its honey. A man who's done good doesn't shout it from the rooftops, but goes on to the next good deed, as a vine goes on to bear grapes again in its season. That's the goal to aim for, to be one of these men oneself, who do good without noticing it, in a way.

---

# — ON —
# FAME

---

People who are overinterested in posthumous fame fail to take into consideration the fact that those who come after them will be no different from those they currently find objectionable, and just as mortal as well. In short, what is it to you what opinions they voice about you or what conception they have of you?

---

Will you be diverted by fame? Focus on the speed with which everything and everyone is forgotten, the infinite temporal gulf that stretches before and after a lifetime, the hollowness of applause, the haphazard fickleness of those who appear to speak well of you, and the narrowness of the place where fame is confined. The whole earth is just a speck. How tiny is the little corner of it where you reside? How many people are there here to praise you? What kind of men will they be?

Anyone who gets excited by the prospect of post-humous fame is failing to realize that all the people who remember him will very shortly be dead themselves, and that the same goes for the next generation in its turn, until the memory is totally extinguished as it progresses from person to person, each of whom is lit and then snuffed out. Even if we posit immortality for the people who are to remember you, and hence for their memories of you, what's that to you? I don't mean just that being remembered is nothing to the dead; I'm asking what good praise does someone while he's alive, unless it serves some further purpose.

Before long, either ashes or a skeleton, and either just a name or not even that—and what's a name but noise and a fading echo?

---

Small too is even the longest-lasting posthumous fame, and it depends on a sequence of little men who will die very soon, and who aren't aware even of themselves, let alone someone who died long ago.

---

How many people who were once world-famous have by now been consigned to oblivion! How many people who once sang their praises have long since departed!

---

Soon you'll have forgotten everything; soon everyone will have forgotten you.

---

So what is valuable? Applause? No. And therefore the same goes for verbal plaudits, seeing that the praise of the multitude is just the clapping of tongues.

---

# — ON —
# FIRST IMPRESSIONS

---

Don't elaborate on what your immediate impressions report. Suppose the report is that so-and-so is maligning you. End of report; nothing in it about your having been harmed. I see that my child is ill; that's what I see, but I don't see that he's in any danger. So always go with your first impressions, adding no extra commentary of your own from within, and you're not affected.

---

# — ON —
# FORGIVENESS

---

When someone mistreats you, the first question you should ask yourself is what conception of good and bad led him to do so. Understanding this will lead you to feel sorry for him, and will dispel any shock or anger, once you see that your own conception of goodness is still either the same as his or closely related. And so you're bound to forgive him. On the other hand, if you've moved beyond this kind of conception of goodness and badness, it will be all the easier for you to be lenient toward him for not seeing things right.

---

# —— ON ——
# FORTITUDE

———

Fortitude, strength, and courage are attributes of a calm and gentle man, not one who's irascible and easily offended, because the closer a man is to being impassive, the closer he is also to being a man of power. Anger is just as much a sign of weakness as suffering is, because both an angry man and a man in pain have surrendered to a wound they've incurred.

———

Every event that takes place either can or can't be endured by you, given your nature. If an event that takes place is within the natural limits of your endurance, don't complain, but put up with it, since you can, given your nature. If it goes beyond those limits, don't complain, because it will simply finish you off. But remember that nature has made you capable of enduring anything, as long as it is up to your judgment to render it endurable and tolerable by representing to yourself the doing of it as either advantageous or your duty.

# — ON —
# THE GODS

When people ask, "But have you ever seen the gods? What makes you so certain of their existence that you revere them like this?," I reply, first, that they are in fact visible and, second, that I haven't seen my soul either, but I'm still in awe of it. So that's how it is with the gods as well: every time I experience their power, I ascertain that they exist and I revere them.

The man who lives with the gods is the one whose soul is constantly on display to them as content with its lot and obedient to the will of the guardian spirit, the fragment of himself that Zeus has granted every person to act as his custodian and command center. And in each of us this is mind and reason.

If the gods deliberated about me and the lot they had in store for me, they came to the right decisions. After all, it isn't easy to conceive of a god who's a poor decision-maker, and why would they intend to do me harm? What would that gain either them or the common good, which is the chief concern of their providence? Even if I personally wasn't the object of their deliberations, they certainly took thought for the common good, and, since what happens to me is a concomitant of that, I'm bound to welcome and embrace these experiences too.

# — ON —
# GRATITUDE

---

Continually call to mind how many doctors have died, after knitting their brows time and again over patients; how many astrologers, after foretelling others' deaths as though death were something important; how many philosophers, after racking their brains about death and immortality; how many great warriors, after having taken numerous other lives; how many tyrants, after exercising the power of life and death with terrible high-handedness, thinking themselves immortal; how many whole towns have died, so to speak—Helice, Pompeii, Herculaneum, and countless others. Recall also people you've personally known, the sequence of them: A saw to B's funeral and was then laid out for his own funeral, which was seen to by C—and it all happened so quickly. In short, always look on human life as transient and worthless; yesterday a bit of slime, tomorrow a mummy or ashes. So spend this fleeting moment of time living in accord with nature, and take your leave with serenity, as a ripe olive might fall blessing the earth that bore it and grateful to the tree that gave it growth.

———

The gods' works are filled with providence; the works of fortune aren't independent of nature or of the interlacing and intertwining of things under the direction of providence. It is the source of everything, including necessity and the well-being of the universe, the whole of which you are a part. What is good for every part of nature is what is supplied by the nature of the whole and what preserves the whole; and what preserves the whole is the changing of the compounds no less than the changing of the physical elements. Be content with these doctrines; make them your constant guiding principles. Get over your thirst for books, so that you don't die grumbling, but with true serenity and with heartfelt gratitude to the gods.

# ── ON ──
# GRIEF

---

Anyone who absconds from a master is a runaway slave. The law is our master, and so anyone who breaks the law is a runaway slave. So is someone who's moved by grief or anger or fear to resent something, past, present, or future, that has been ordained by the power that directs the universe, which is law, the law that assigns our due to each of us. So anyone who's being moved by fear or grief or anger is a runaway slave.

---

When someone has been bitten by true principles, even a very brief and hackneyed prompt can serve as a reminder to dispel sorrow and fear. For instance: "The wind scatters the leaves on the ground; such is the race of men." Your children too are mere leaves.

Tragedies were originally produced as reminders of what happens in the world—to call attention to the fact that these events are natural and that what you find attractive in the theater should not cause you sorrow on the larger stage of life.

# — ON —
# HEALTH AND
# ILLNESS

This is from Epicurus: "During my illness, I didn't make my physical suffering a topic of conversation, or talk about anything like that to visitors. Instead, I continued to talk as a natural scientist, expounding my principal doctrines, and focusing especially on this very point, how the mind, despite the fact that it shares in such physical disturbances, remains unperturbed and preserves its specific good. Nor," he goes on, "did I let my doctors get all bigheaded as if they were doing something important. I just got on with my life as well and nicely as usual." You should do the same as him when you're ill (if you happen to be ill) and in all other circumstances.

---

A healthy eye must see all that is visible and not say, "No bright colors, please!" That would be a symptom of an eye infection. A healthy ear or nose must be ready for everything that can be heard or smelled. A healthy stomach must be similarly ready for everything edible, as a mill is ready for everything it's been made to grind. And so a healthy mind must be ready for everything that happens, but a mind that says, "I hope my children are safe," or, "I'd like to be praised by everyone for everything I do," is like an eye that wants only pale colors or teeth that want only soft foods.

---

# — ON —
# HELPING OTHERS

If you can, get them to mend their ways, and if you can't, remember that this is exactly why you've been endowed with kindness. Even the gods are kind to such people and help them achieve some of their objectives—health, wealth, prestige. That's how good they are. You can do it too. Or tell me: Who's stopping you?

Don't get completely carried away by their thoughts, but give as much help as you can and as the situation deserves, even if the loss they're suffering involves nothing of moral significance. But don't think that they're *really* being harmed; that would be a bad habit to get into. You should behave like the old man who went off to demand the return of his foster child's whirligig, even though he was well aware that it was only a toy. Have you forgotten, my friend, how little these things are worth? "Yes, but they're of great importance to these people." Well, is that any reason for you to behave like an idiot as well?

# — ON —
# HONESTY AND
# DISHONESTY

---

Salvation in life comes from always seeing everything as it really is, by distinguishing its matter and its cause, and from wholeheartedly doing right and speaking truth. Then all that's left is to enjoy a life of linking one good deed with another, leaving not the slightest gap between them.

---

If it's not right, don't do it; if it's not the truth, don't say it. Your impulses should be under your control.

———

Although they despise one another, they behave obsequiously to one another; although they want to overshadow one another, they grovel to one another.

———

How corrupt and devious is a man who says, "I've decided to be straight with you"! What are you up to, man? There's no need for this preamble; the facts will speak for themselves. Your face should be an open book. Honesty is immediately clear from the tone of voice and the look in the eyes, just as a loved one immediately knows everything from his admirers' glances. In short, a good, sincere person must resemble a stinking goatherd, in the sense that anyone who comes close to him should, willy-nilly, immediately be aware what he's like. But calculated sincerity is like a concealed blade. There's nothing more shameful than wolf-friendship; there's nothing more important than avoiding it. The eyes of a man who's good, sincere, and kind reveal what he's like, and you can't mistake him.

Perfection of character lies in this: to live each day as though it were your last, without turmoil, without listlessness, and without pretense.

———

So what should one take seriously? Only the following: a just mind, socially useful actions, speech that only ever tells the truth, and the ability to welcome everything that happens as necessary, as comprehensible by reason, and as flowing from an equally rational original source.

———

# — ON —
# HUMAN NATURE

A person's lifetime is a moment, his existence a
flowing stream, his perception dull, the entire
fabric of his body readily subject to decay, his
soul an aimless wanderer, his fortune erratic, his
fame uncertain. In short: the body is nothing but
a river; the soul is dream and delusion; life is war
and a sojourn in a strange land; and oblivion is
all there is to posthumous fame. What, then, can
escort us safely on our way? Only one thing: philosophy. This consists in keeping the guardian

spirit within us safe from assault and harm, never swayed by pleasure or pain, purposeful when it acts, free from dishonesty or dissemblance, and never dependent on action or inaction from anyone else. It also consists in accepting what happens, the lot one has been assigned, as coming from the same source as oneself, and in always awaiting death with a serene mind, understanding that it's no more than the disintegration of the elements of which every living creature is a compound. If there's nothing unusual in the elements themselves changing moment by moment one into another, why should the alteration and disintegration of them all be a cause for anxiety? It's in accord with nature, and nothing that's in accord with nature is bad.

Here are things you should always bear in mind: what the nature of the whole is; what my nature is; how my nature is related to the nature of the whole; what kind of part it is of what kind of whole; and that no one is stopping you from being in accord with the nature of which you are a part, in all you ever say or do.

A human being should pay no attention to things that aren't proper to him qua human. Such things make no demands of him as a human being, nor are they guaranteed by his nature as a human being, nor do they fulfill human nature. So the end of human life isn't located in them either, nor are they good, because goodness is what the end of human life is all about. Moreover, if any of them were proper to him as a human being, it wouldn't be proper for him to scorn and resist them, nor would we find it commendable to have no need of them, nor, if they were good, would someone who was without any of them be a good person. But, in fact, the more someone deprives himself of them or other similar things, or even allows himself to be deprived of them, the better a person he is.

# — ON —
# THE INTERIOR
# CASTLE

---

An impassive mind is a citadel. A man can have no better stronghold where he can take refuge and remain unassailable.

---

People try to find retreats for themselves in the countryside, by the sea, and in the mountains. A marked longing for such a haven has been a habit of yours too. But nothing could be more unphilosophical, given that you may retreat into yourself whenever you want. There's no retreat more peaceful and untroubled than a man's own mind.

---

Remember that you already have a little estate into which you can retreat, and make it your priority not to get agitated or tense. Better to be your own master.

---

Withdraw into yourself. It's natural for the command center to be content with the justice of its actions and with the tranquility it has as a result.

# — ON —
# JUSTICE

---

"Whatever happens, it's right that it should happen." If you observe things carefully, you'll find this to be the case. When I say that it's right, I don't mean merely that it plays its part in the universal sequence of cause and effect, but that it's consistent with justice—as though there were someone rewarding things as they deserved.

Where it's within your power to consider what has to be done, there's no need for guesswork. If you can see the way forward, take it without turning aside, and if you can't, hold back and consult your best advisers. If you meet with obstacles, make use of the resources you have and proceed cautiously, keeping always to the course that seems to you to be just. For there's nothing better than the attainment of justice, since the only real failure is falling short of justice.

Imperturbability in the face of things that are externally caused; justice in all activity that is initiated by yourself.

First, don't be upset. Nothing happens that isn't in accord with universal nature, and before long you won't exist at all, just like Hadrian and Augustus. Second, fix your gaze on the matter in hand and see it for what it is, and then, keeping in mind your obligation to be a good person and the demands of your humanity, go right ahead and do it, in the way that seems to you to be most just. But do it with kindness and modesty, and without dissembling.

# — ON —
# KINDNESS

---

Is someone going to despise me? That's his concern. Mine is to see that I don't do or say anything that deserves to be despised. Is someone going to hate me? That's his concern. I'll remain kind and benevolent to everyone. I'll also be ready to show this particular person what he's overlooking, not harshly and not as a way of flaunting my patience, but genuinely and tactfully.

———

With right reason as your guide, those who stand in your way will be unable to deflect you from a sound course of action, but you mustn't let them force you to renounce your kindness to them. You must be equally on your guard in both respects. You need to make sure not only that your decisions and actions are unshakable, but also that you continue to be gentle toward those who try to thwart you or cause you grief in some other way. Treating them harshly would be no less a sign of weakness than abandoning a course of action and being cowed into giving up.

———

Try living the life of a good man and see how it suits you—a man who's gratified by the lot he's been assigned by the universe and satisfied with the justice of his acts and the kindness of his character.

———

How have you behaved up until now toward gods, parents, siblings, wife, children, teachers, tutors, friends, family, and slaves? Check whether toward all of them so far your principle has been "Do no evil and speak no evil."

———

# — ON —
# KINSHIP

It's typically human to feel affection even for people who make mistakes. The feeling is a response to the thoughts that they're your kin, that they're led astray against their will by their ignorance, that shortly both of you will be dead, and especially that he did you no harm, because he didn't make your command center worse than it was before.

Anything that shares some essential quality with other things seeks its own kind. Everything earthy sinks earthward, everything watery merges with other liquids, and the same goes for airy things. And so everything that partakes of intelligent nature similarly seeks its own kind. Or rather, it has an even stronger predisposition to do so, because to the extent that it's superior to the other things I've mentioned, it's that much more ready to commingle and blend with what is like it.

At any rate, from the very beginning, among irrational creatures there existed swarms, flocks, the feeding of young, and something like love, because there were, after all, souls involved, and at this higher level there was a tendency to unity of an intensity not to be found in plants or stones or logs. In rational creatures, this same tendency manifests as communities, friendships, households, assemblies, and treaties and truces at times of war. And among still higher beings there exists a kind of unity consisting of discrete things, such as one finds among the heavenly bodies. Thus the higher up the scale one goes, the greater the possibility there is of an interactive connection being forged even among discrete things.

Now compare the world at present. Currently, intelligent creatures are alone in having consigned to oblivion the urge to unity with one another. Only here is the merging of like with like something one never sees. But, run from it as they might, it still catches up with them. Such is the power of nature. If you pay attention, you'll get the point. I mean, you're more likely to find earthy things separated from one another than a human being who's cut off from other human beings.

———

# — ON —
# LAZINESS

Whenever you find it difficult to wake up, remind yourself that doing socially useful work is proper to your constitution and your humanity, while sleeping is something you share with irrational animals as well. And anything that's proper to an individual's nature has greater affinity to him and is second nature to him—and, moreover, is more refreshing.

At dawn, when you're reluctant to get up, have this thought readily available: I have work to do as a human being, and that's why I'm getting up. Do I still resent it if I'm on my way to do the work for which I was born and for the sake of which I was brought into the world? Or is *this* what I was made for, to lie in bed and keep myself warm? "But it's really nice." So is pleasure what you were born for? And, in general, was it for feeling, not for doing? Can't you see plants, sparrows, ants, spiders, and bees all doing their own work and playing their part in the world's order? And are you then reluctant to do human work? Why aren't you eager to do what comes naturally to you?

"But rest is important too." Yes, I agree. Nature has set limits on rest, however, as it has on eating and drinking as well; but aren't you overstepping those limits and taking more than suffices for your needs? It's only when it comes to action that you haven't yet reached the limits of your abilities. And the reason is that you don't love yourself. If you did, you'd love your nature and its purpose. Other people who are devoted to their areas of expertise wear themselves out over them, forgetting to wash or eat. Do you value your own nature less than an artisan does his metalwork, a dancer his dancing, a miser his money, a celebrity his moment of fame? In their obsession, they're willing to give up food and sleep in favor of spending more time over the objects of their passion. Does state business seem less important to you, worth less effort than they put in?

———

# — ON — LEADERSHIP

First, never act without plan and purpose. Second, set your sights on no other goal but the common good.

"A king's role is to do good and be reviled."

You should be ever ready in two respects. First, to act only as the reason embodied in the arts of kingship and lawmaking proposes, for the benefit of humanity. Second, to change your mind if there happens to be someone around to correct you and steer you away from any form of presumption. But the change must always be founded on a conviction that the outcome will be just, or will enhance the welfare of the state, and you must only ever act in ways that contribute to such outcomes, without taking pleasure or popularity into account.

Don't expect to create Plato's ideal state, but be satisfied if you make even the slightest progress, and regard that in itself as no small achievement.

---

Beware of becoming Caesarified, dyed in purple. It does happen. Keep yourself simple, good, guileless, dignified, unpretentious, devoted to justice, pious, kind, affectionate to others, and resolute in carrying out your proper tasks. Strive to be and remain the kind of person philosophy would have you be. Revere the gods and keep men safe. Life is short. There's only one crop to be reaped from your time on earth, and that is a reverential disposition and socially useful actions.

---

Anything which isn't good for the hive isn't good for the bee either.

---

If sailors criticized their helmsman or invalids their doctor, wouldn't their only concern be how he might ensure the safety of his crew or the health of his patients?

---

# ON
# LOSS

Accept graciously, let go easily.

Loss is just change, and change pleases universal nature, which is responsible for everything that comes to pass and for the goodness of everything that comes to pass. Good things have happened from eternity, and there will be more in the infinite future. Why, then, do you say that every-thing that has happened and will happen is bad, that none of the host of gods has the power to correct the situation, and that the world has been condemned to be unremittingly afflicted by evil?

# — ON —
# LUCK

---

"Once I was a lucky man, wherever I was to be found." But a lucky man is one who makes his own good fortune, and good fortune consists in good uses of the mind, good impulses, and good deeds.

---

Be like a headland: the waves beat against it continuously, but it stands fast and around it the boiling water dies down. "It's my rotten luck that this has happened to me." On the contrary: "It's my good luck that, although this has happened to me, I still feel no distress, since I'm unbruised by the present and unconcerned about the future." What happened could have happened to anyone, but not everyone could have carried on without letting it distress him. So why regard the incident as a piece of bad luck, rather than seeing your avoidance of distress as a piece of good luck? Do you generally describe a person as unlucky when his nature worked well? Do you count it as a malfunction of a person's nature when it succeeds in securing the outcome it wanted? Well, you know from your studies what it is that human nature wants. Can what happened to you stop you from being fair, high-minded, moderate, conscientious, unhasty, honest, moral, self-reliant, and so on—from possessing all the qualities which, when present, enable a man's nature to be fulfilled? So then, whenever something happens that might cause you distress, remember to rely on this principle: this is not bad luck, but bearing it valiantly is good luck.

---

# ON
# OBJECTIVITY

---

Keep all time and all being constantly before your mind, and see that, in terms of being, every individual thing is no more than a fig seed, and in terms of time no more than a twist of a drill.

---

Make it a systematic practice to consider how all things change into one another, pay constant attention to the changing, and train yourself in this respect. Nothing is more conducive to objectivity. A man who looks at things objectively divests himself of his body. He knows that very shortly he'll have to leave all this behind when he departs from the world, and so he commits himself wholly to justice in his own actions and entrusts himself to universal nature when it comes to events that are beyond his control. It never occurs to him to wonder what people will say or think about him, or what they'll do against him, but he's content, first, if he always does what is right, and, second, if he embraces his lot in its entirety. He gives up every distraction and diversion, and all he wants is to continue straight on the path of law and thereby to follow God.

How useful it is, when you're served roast meat and similar dishes, to think to yourself: this is the corpse of a fish, this is the corpse of a bird or a pig! Or again, to see Falernian wine as mere grape juice, your purple-hemmed cloak as sheep's wool dyed with shellfish blood, and sexual intercourse as just the rubbing of an organ and the spasm-induced emission of a little slime. How good these thoughts are at reaching and getting to the heart of things! They enable you to see things for what they are. This should be a lifelong exercise: whenever things particularly seem to deserve your acceptance, strip them bare so that you can see how worthless they are and dispense with the descriptions that make them seem more significant than they are.

What a tiny fraction of the infinite gulf of time has been allotted to each of us! It's very quickly swallowed up by eternity. What a tiny fraction of the entirety of substance! What a tiny fraction of the entirety of soul! What a tiny clod of earth you crawl on, compared to the earth as a whole! Bear all this in mind and think nothing important except acting in compliance with your nature and being acted upon by whatever universal nature brings your way.

---

Take a look from on high and what do you see? Countless herds, countless ceremonies, voyages of every kind being undertaken in storm and calm, the endless variety of people being born, living together, passing away. Think also of the lives lived by others in the past, the lives that will be lived after you, and the lives that are being lived today by peoples of foreign lands. See how many there are who don't even know your name, how many of them will very soon forget you, and how many of them may be praising you now, but will very soon be denouncing you. Recognize that neither memory nor fame nor anything else at all has any importance.

---

If you were suddenly in a position to look down from on high on human life in all its chaotic diversity, you'd find it singularly unimpressive, because you'd simultaneously be seeing all around yourself the great company of beings who populate the air and the aether; and that however many times you were raised aloft what you'd see would never change; it would just be the same old ephemeral things. And these are what we deluded beings consider important!

There's one point yet to add to the above reminders. Always define or describe to yourself every impression that occurs to your mind, so that you can clearly see what the thing is like in its entirety, stripped to its essence, and tell yourself its proper name and the names of the elements of which it consists and into which it will be resolved. Nothing is more conducive to objectivity than the ability methodically and honestly to test everything that you come across in life, and always to look at things in such a way that you consider what kind of part each of them plays in what kind of universe, and what value it has for the universe as a whole and for a man who is a citizen of the highest state, the state of which all other states are, so to speak, mere households.

Constantly bear in mind how everything that's happening now happened also in the past. Bear in mind too that it will all happen in the future as well—entire plays with the same kinds of scenes, already familiar to you from your experience or from history books. Visualize them: for example, the whole of Hadrian's court, or that of Philip or Alexander or Croesus. The scenes were all the same, though played by different actors.

# —— ON ——
# OLD AGE

———————

One must take into consideration not only the fact that life is being used up day by day and there's less of it left, but also that, if one were to live longer, there's no guarantee that one's mind will remain unaffected and capable of understanding the way things are in themselves, or the concepts that guide one's experience of matters both divine and human. The early symptoms of senility don't involve the failure of things like transpiration, digestion, sense perception, or impulse; the first to go are abilities that require a well-trained mental faculty, such as making proper use of oneself, accurately estimating the limits of appropriate behavior, analyzing one's impressions, and understanding whether the time has come to take your leave of this life. You must have a sense of urgency, then, not only because at each moment you're drawing closer to death, but also because your understanding of the world around you and your ability to pay attention to it will come to an end before you do.

———

It's high time now for you to recognize that a limit has been set on your time, and if you don't use it to dispel the mists it will pass, and you will pass, and the opportunity won't come again.

———

The light of a lamp shines and continues to shed light until it's extinguished. Will the truth, justice, and moderation in you be extinguished before their time?

---

Remind yourself what you've been through and what you've had the strength to endure, and that the story of your life is now coming to an end, your service completed. Remind yourself of all the admirable deeds you've witnessed, how many times you've overcome pleasure and pain, how many distinctions you've disdained, and how many discourteous people you've treated with courtesy.

---

It's horrible that in this life, while your body keeps going, your mind gives up first.

———

Your death is imminent, and you haven't yet achieved simplicity, imperturbability, the conviction that nothing external can make you a worse person, or the ability to deal serenely with everyone, nor do you dedicate your intelligence solely to right action.

———

# — ON —
# PAIN AND
# DISTRESS

---

Pain is a negative experience that is either physical (in which case the body is entitled to protest) or mental. But the mind can preserve its own clarity and tranquility by refusing to take pain to be bad. For every judgment, impulse, desire, and aversion is internal, and nothing bad intrudes there.

Remove the belief and "I've been harmed" goes as well; remove "I've been harmed" and the harm goes as well.

———

If you get rid of the belief about what seems to be hurting you, you stand in an absolutely hurt-free place. "Which 'you'?" Reason. "But I'm not reason." All right. So reason won't cause itself pain, and any other part of you that's suffering is welcome to believe that about itself.

———

---

Whenever you're in pain, have this thought readily available: it isn't a shameful thing, nor does it impair the mind that holds the helm. Pain has no deleterious effect on the mind qua rational, nor qua concerned for the common good. As far as most instances of pain are concerned, there's a useful saying of Epicurus: "Pain is either not unendurable or not everlasting"—as long as you remember that it has limits and as long as you don't judge it further. And remember this too, that there are plenty of disagreeable feelings that are the same as pain, even if we might not realize it, such as drowsiness, heat exhaustion, and loss of appetite. So when one of these is making you miserable, tell yourself that you're giving in to pain.

---

If something external is causing you distress, it's not the thing itself that's troubling you, but your judgment about it, and it's within your power to erase that right now. And if it's something internal to yourself, is anyone stopping you from looking at it in a more positive way? Likewise, if you're distressed because you're failing to do something that strikes you as sound, why not do it rather than indulge in distress? "But the obstacle is too strong for me." In that case, there's no need for distress, because you're not responsible for your inability to act.

# — ON —
# PEACE OF MIND

---

Remember that it's not people's actions that disturb our peace of mind (because their actions are the business of their own command centers), but our own opinions of their actions. At any rate, eliminate the judgment that they're doing something hurtful, and be willing to let go of it, and anger comes to an end.

---

Your peace of mind is disturbed by the pursuit or avoidance of things, but these things don't force themselves on you; in a sense, you force yourself on them.

———

Pick me up and throw me where you will. Wherever it is, I shall preserve the serenity of my guardian spirit, or in other words its contentment with its condition and its activity, given their compatibility with its own constitution. Is there anything about the present situation that justifies my soul's being in a bad way and out of sorts—depressed, yearning, constrained, scared? In fact, do you think there's *any* situation which would justify that?

———

When the pressure of circumstances somewhat disturbs your peace of mind, recover quickly and don't lose your rhythm for longer than necessary. In any case, you'll master the measure all the better by constantly returning to it.

———

The command center doesn't disturb itself, by which I mean that it doesn't alarm itself, distress itself, or give in to desire. If anyone else is able to alarm or distress it, that's up to him; the command center will not of its own accord cause any such worsening of itself.

———

No more making your life miserable by grumbling and playing the ape! Why disturb your peace of mind? There's nothing new here, is there? What is it that's upsetting you? Its cause? See it for what it is. Its matter, perhaps? See it for what it is. Apart from cause and matter, there's nothing else. By the gods, become a simpler and better person, and do it now! Three years is as good as a hundred for this quest.

# ON
# PHILOSOPHY

---

If you had both a stepmother and a mother, you'd do your duty by your stepmother, and yet you'd constantly return to your mother. That's how you stand today in relation to the imperial court and philosophy. Return, then, at frequent intervals to philosophy and lean on it for rest. With its help, even court business seems tolerable to you, and you become tolerable while attending to it.

---

Don't give up in disgust or weariness if your ability to act consistently on the basis of right principles doesn't consolidate into a permanent habit. After every repulse, go back, and be happy if the majority of your actions are worthy of a human being. And hold it dear, what you're going back to. Don't return to philosophy as a child to a teacher, but as someone with an eye infection turns to the swab and the eyecup, or as another turns to his bandage and poultice. Then you'll be showing that compliance with reason is no burden, but a relief. Remember that philosophy wants only what your nature wants, and that it was you who were wanting something else, that was not in accord with nature. And what could be more delightful than satisfying your nature's wants?

# — ON —
# PLEASURE

---

Everything—a horse, for instance, or a vine—has come into existence for some purpose. Is there anything surprising in that? Even the sun would say, "I was born to do a certain job," and so would the other gods. So what's *your* purpose in life? To experience pleasure? Is that a sustainable idea, do you think?

---

It's sacrilegious for what is rational and contributes to the common good to be rivaled by anything that is different in kind, such as popularity, political power, wealth, or sensual pleasure—all things that afford a brief illusion of happiness, but then suddenly overpower one and lead one astray. So, as I say, you must simply and freely choose the better course and stay with it. "But what is better is what does me good." If it does you good as a rational being, don't dispense with it; but if it does you good as an animal, spurn it and keep to your original decision.

Regret is a kind of censure of oneself for having missed a favorable opportunity. Anything favorable is bound to be good and should be of interest to every upright and good man. But no such man would regret having missed an opportunity for pleasure. It follows that pleasure is neither favorable nor good.

# — ON —
# POSSESSIONS

What follows is a way of understanding the kinds of things that are taken to be good by ordinary people. If one were thinking of the possession of things that are truly good (such as wisdom, moderation, justice, and courage), with those on his mind he wouldn't be able to make sense of the saying about being "crowded by good things," because it wouldn't apply. However, if he were thinking of the things ordinary people take to be good, he'll get the playwright's point and see its appropriateness.

So even ordinary people glimpse the difference between the two sets of goods, because otherwise the saying wouldn't cause offense and attract criticism, while we accept it as a pointed and humorous comment on wealth and the blessings associated with luxury or prestige. Then next you need to ask whether it's right for one to value and regard as good things of which, when we have them on our minds, it can appropriately be said that their possessor is so well off "that he has no place to shit!"

———

Instead of imagining that you possess things you don't, select, from among those you *do* have, the ones you count yourself most fortunate to have, and remind yourself in their case how much you'd have wanted them if you didn't have them. But at the same time take care not to let your pleasure in them get you into the habit of valuing them too highly, to the extent that you'd be upset if you ever lost them.

———

# — ON —
# PRAISE

What do you think of someone who courts the approval of, or noise generated by, people who applaud while having no idea where they are or who they are?

Do you want to be praised by a man who curses himself three times an hour? Do you want to be liked by a man who doesn't like himself? If a man regrets almost everything he does, can he be said to like himself?

---

How presumptuous of them to imagine that they're hurting you with their criticism or doing you good by singing your praises!

---

# — ON —
# PRAYER

---

An Athenian prayer: "Rain, Zeus, please. Rain on the farmland and the fields of the Athenians." That's how to pray, simply and in a spirit of self-reliance; otherwise, one shouldn't pray at all.

---

The gods are either powerless or powerful. If they have no power, what's the point of prayer? And if they do have power, isn't it preferable to pray for them to grant the ability not to fear or desire or be hurt by anything, rather than asking to have this or not have that? I mean, there's no doubt that, if the gods have the power to help human beings, they can help in these respects. You might respond by saying: "The gods have made these things 'up to me,' so isn't it better for you to manage in a self-reliant way the things that are up to you, rather than being concerned in a servile and submissive way with things that aren't up to you?" But from where did you get the idea that the gods don't also help with things that are up to us? Anyway, start praying for these things, and you'll see for yourself. One man's prayer is "Help me to bed that woman," while yours is "Help me not to desire to bed that woman." Another's is "Help me get rid of that man," while yours is "Help me not to want to get rid of that man." Another's is "Help me not to lose my child," while yours is "Help me not to be afraid of losing my child." In short, turn your prayers around like that and see what happens.

_____

# ON
# THE PRESENT

Even if you were to live for three thousand years or ten times as long, remember that the only life anyone loses is this one, the one he's living, and the only life anyone lives is the one he loses. It follows that the longest life and the shortest life come to the same thing. The present moment is equal for all, and therefore its passing is equal for all, and therefore what is lost turns out to be a mere instant. After all, no one can lose either the past or the future, because no one can lose what they don't have. Bear in mind, then, that both the longest-lived and the shortest-lived lose an equal amount of time, because the present is the only thing one can lose, since that is all one has, and no one can lose what they don't have.

———————

Wherever you find yourself, it's within your power, at every moment, to be reverently content with your present circumstances, to behave with justice toward the people presently around you, and to manage your present impressions so that nothing slips into your mind that you haven't adequately grasped.

———————

Living is more like wrestling than dancing: one should stand ready for every contingency and avoid being thrown even by unforeseen developments.

---

All those qualities that you pray to get in the due course of time—you can have them now if you don't deny yourself them. What you have to do is leave the past behind, entrust the future to providence, and, focusing on the present alone, direct it toward piety and justice: piety, so that you embrace your lot, seeing that it was nature that brought you to it and it to you; and justice, so that you speak the truth without restriction or equivocation, and act in conformity with law and equity. Don't let anything stand in your way, such as someone else's iniquity, or what people think or say, or, of course, the sensations of your casing, the body.

---

Remember that each of us lives only in the fleeting present moment, and that all the rest of our lives has either already been lived or is undisclosed.

---

Beware of the disquiet that can follow from picturing your life as a whole. Don't dwell on all the various kinds of troubles that have happened and are likely to happen in the future as well. No, focus on the present, and ask yourself whether there's anything about the task before you that's unbearable and insupportable, because it would be shameful to admit that there is. And then remind yourself that neither the future nor the past can weigh on you, but only the present, and that the present becomes easier to bear if you take it on its own; and rebuke your mind if it's too feeble to endure something that's so uncluttered.

# — ON —
# PROVIDENCE

Honor the greatest power in the universe; every-thing and everyone are its instruments and sub-jects. By the same token, honor the greatest power in yourself as well. It's the same in kind as that universal power, since the same goes for you too: all your parts are its instruments and your life is under its direction.

Don't upset yourself; don't complicate your life. Is someone treating you badly? He's doing it to himself. Has something happened to you? Good: every one of your experiences has been ordained and fated for you from the beginning by the universe.

———

There's no real difference between saying, "Asclepius prescribed horse riding for him, or cold baths, or walking barefoot," and, "The universe prescribed illness for him, or mutilation, or wasting, or some other affliction." In the first sentence, "prescribed" means something like "instructed him to do such-and-such as conducive to his health," and in the second sentence the meaning is that a person's experiences have somehow been ordained for him as conducive to his destiny.

———

# — ON —
# REASON

---

A human being bears fruit as well, so does God, and so does the universe. Each of them is productive in its own season. Never mind if convention has reduced the proper usage of the word to vines and so on. Reason too has its fruit, both general and particular, and its issue consists of more things of the same kind as itself.

---

An arrow moves in one way, the mind in another. But even when the mind exercises caution and circles around an object of investigation, it's still moving straight for its target.

———

"Are you endowed with reason?" Yes, I am. "Why don't you use it, then? I mean, if it's doing its job, what else can you want?"

———

The properties of the rational soul: it sees itself; it elucidates itself; it makes of itself whatever it wants to be; it gathers its own fruit (whereas the fruit of plants and the equivalent in animals are gathered by others); it achieves its end at whatever point life may come to a close. Unlike a dance or a play or something like that, where if the performance is cut off at any point the production as a whole is incomplete, the rational soul fully and completely finishes every one of its projects, whatever scene is being played.

If intelligence is something we have in common, then reason too, which makes us rational beings, is something we have in common. If so, then the reason that dictates what we should and shouldn't do is also something we have in common. If so, then law too is something we have in common. If so, then we're fellow citizens. If so, then we have some form of society in common. If so, then the world is a kind of community, since the world is the only shared society that anyone could describe as common to the entire human race. And it's from there, from this shared community, in fact, that we get intelligence, reason, and law. I mean, where else could they come from? After all, just as the earthy part of me is a fragment of some earth, and the watery part of me is a fragment of another element, and the airy part has come from some source, and the hot, fiery part has come from *its* own specific source—for nothing comes from nothing, just as nothing returns to nothing—so our intelligence too has come from somewhere.

———

Don't you see how common artisans adjust their work to a certain extent to suit nonspecialists, but still stay just as true as ever to the rational principle of their art and hate to abandon it? Isn't it shocking, then, for a builder and a doctor to respect the rational principle of their crafts more than a person respects his own rational principle, which is common to him and the gods?

———

———

Reason and the art of reasoning form a closed system between themselves and their results. They set out from their own proper starting point and make their way to the designated goal. That's why rational actions are called "right actions," as a way of indicating that they keep us on the right path.

———

Don't be anxious about the future. You'll come to it (if you must), equipped with the same reason that you apply now to the present.

———

You can always be content if you continue to make good progress, which is to say if your beliefs and actions keep you on the path of reason. There are two features which are common to the minds of gods, men, and any other rational beings there may be: they are immune to external obstruction, and what they count as good is right thinking and right action, which they make the limit of their desire.

What every individual creature has to do is what follows from its constitution, and although all other beings have been created to serve rational ones (and it's a universal principle that the lower serves the higher), rational beings are made to serve one another. So the leading principle in the human constitution is concern for the common good, and the second is resistance to bodily feelings. For it's typical of rational and intelligent activity to be self-contained and never overcome by the activity of either the senses or the impulses. The point is that sensations and impulses belong to our animal nature, while it's the aim of intelligent activity not to surrender its leadership and be overcome by them. And that's how it should be, because it's in its nature to make use of sensations and impulses for its own purposes.

# — ON —
# THE RULER
# WITHIN

---

In its natural state, the situation of the ruler within us as regards the events of the world is such that it readily adapts itself to what's feasible. It isn't wedded to any particular material that's proper specifically to it, but sets out with reservation to achieve its objectives, and converts everything that it encounters into material for itself. It's like a bonfire overpowering the objects that are thrown onto it; a small fire would be extinguished by them, but a good blaze very quickly appropriates to itself all the objects that are piled on it, consumes them, and uses them to grow greater.

---

Remember that the puppet master controlling your strings is the power hidden within you. Without it, there's no activity, no life—no person, one might even say. When you think of it, be sure never to confuse it with the vessel that contains it and the organs that have been molded around it. They're tools, like an adze, with the only difference being that they're conjoined with us. After all, the fact of the matter is that none of these parts is any more use to us without the cause that starts and stops it than a shuttle is without a weaver, a pen without a writer, or a whip without a carter.

---

# — ON —
# THE SACRED
# BOND

———

All things are interwoven with one another. The bond that unites them is sacred, and it's hardly an exaggeration to say that nothing is alien to anything else, because they've been formed into a collaborative system, and together they contribute to the orderliness of the same universe. After all, the universe, being made up of all there is, is one, and the God who permeates everything is one, and there's one reality, one law, one reason that's common to all intelligent creatures, and one truth—that is, if there's just one way in which beings that are related and share the same reason can be fulfilled.

---

Just as doctors always keep their instruments and implements ready to hand for emergency procedures, so you should keep your principles ready for understanding the divine and human realms, and everything you do, however trivial, should be done with consciousness of the bond that unites the two realms, in the sense that you won't succeed on the human level without simultaneously aiming at the divine, or vice versa.

---

# — ON —
# SELF-AWARENESS

One doesn't commonly see people becoming miserable as a result of not taking note of what's going on in someone else's soul, but anyone who's unaware of the activity of his own soul can't help but be miserable.

There's nothing more pathetic than a man who's always running around and poking his nose in everywhere—investigating "the nether regions of the earth," in the poet's words—and using outside signs to infer what's going on in his neighbors' souls, without realizing that all he needs to do is focus on his own inner guardian spirit and take proper care of it. Caring for it is keeping it unsullied by emotion, purposelessness, and dissatisfaction with the activities of gods and men; for the goodness of the gods is such that their acts are to be respected, and human kinship means that people's acts are to be welcomed. There are times, however, when human acts are also rather pitiful because of their ignorance of good and bad, which is as much of a disability as being blind to the difference between white and black.

# ON
# SELF-SUFFICIENCY

Treat yourself with contempt, soul of mine—yes, contempt! The time has passed for you to respect yourself. For no one lives long, and this life of yours is all but spent while you dishonor yourself and make your happiness depend on the souls of others.

---

Live your whole life unswayed by outside forces and with a wholly joyful heart, even if everyone else is crying out against you and wild beasts are tearing limb from limb this lump of paste that has been caked around you. After all, is there anything in all this that makes it impossible for the mind to maintain its tranquility, or its ability to judge situations correctly, or its facility at making good use of the circumstances with which it is presented?

---

Be joyful within and in need of no external assistance or peace provided by others. You must stand straight, not be straightened.

---

---

To the glory-hunter's way of thinking, what's good for him is others' activity, while for the hedonist it's his own feelings. For an intelligent man, however, it's what he himself does.

---

How much freedom is gained if a man ignores what his neighbor said or did or intended, and considers only what he himself is doing and how to make his actions just and right, the kinds of things a good man would do! Don't let your attention be caught by the darkness of others' humors; just run straight on the line, with no ungainly movements.

---

If you find anything better in human life than justice, honesty, moderation, and courage—if, to put it generally, you find anything better than the self-sufficiency of your mind on those occasions when it ensures that your actions are compatible with right reason, as well as when something is allotted to you by fate without your having chosen it—if, I say, you're aware of anything better than this, turn to it with all your heart and enjoy the supreme good you've discovered. But if you find nothing better than the guardian spirit lodged within you, which has brought all your particular impulses under its control, which scrutinizes your thoughts, which, as Socrates used to say, has withdrawn itself from sensations, which has put itself in the gods' hands, and which cares providentially for other people—if everything else turns out to be trivial and worthless by comparison, then make room for nothing else.

# — ON —
# SOCIABILITY

If you've ever seen a dismembered hand or foot, or a head hacked off and lying somewhere apart from the rest of the body—well, a man does his best to make himself like that if he refuses to accept his lot and cuts himself off from society or behaves selfishly. At some point, you've made yourself an outcast from the unity that's natural to you by virtue of the fact that you became a part of it at birth.

A branch cut off from its neighboring branch is, of course, cut off from the whole tree. In the same way, a human being who's cut off from even one other human being has fallen away from society as a whole. In the case of a branch, it's someone else who does the cutting, but the separation of a man from his neighbor is his own doing, the result of hating him and spurning him, and he fails to realize that he has at the same time severed himself from the community as a whole. But we've been granted a great boon by Zeus, the founder of human society: we can graft ourselves back on to our neighbor and again become component parts of the whole. However, the more often such separation happens, the harder it becomes for the part that withdraws to be reunited and restored to its position.

———

Treat irrational animals, and things and objects in general, in a detached and generous manner, since you have the faculty of reason and they don't. Treat human beings, who do have the faculty of reason, in a sociable manner. And in all things call on the gods for help, and never worry how much time you will have to act in this way; even three hours of such a life is enough.

———

Precisely because you personally are part of the whole that is the body politic, every one of your actions should contribute to a life the purpose of which is to improve society. Any action of yours, then, which doesn't closely or remotely take as its reference point the goal of improving society creates a rupture in your life and prevents it from having integrity, and is just as socially divisive as when a member of a community takes it upon himself to detach himself from the common concord.

# — ON —
# THE SOUL

---

To what use am I now putting my soul? That's the question to ask yourself all the time. And you should interrogate yourself: at this moment, what is occupying that part of me they call the command center? What kind of a soul do I actually have at the moment? Is it the soul of a child? A teenager? A woman? A tyrant? A farm animal? A wild animal?

---

The human soul dishonors itself, first and fore-most, when it becomes, to the extent that it can, a growth and a tumor, as it were, on the universe. To resent anything that happens is to set oneself apart from nature, of which the various individual natures of everything else are parts. A second case is when it rejects another human being or even opposes him with malicious intent; this is what the souls of angry people are like. Third, it dishonors itself when it's defeated by pleasure or pain. Fourth, when it dissembles and does or says anything in an affected or dishonest manner. Fifth, when it fails to direct any of its actions or impulses toward a goal, but instead acts without purpose and without attention, when even the slightest actions should be carried out with reference to the end.

---

The things of the world cannot affect the soul; they lie inert outside it, and only internal beliefs can disturb it.

---

Clear your mind; control your impulses; extinguish desire; see that your command center retains its self-mastery.

---

Sunlight is single, even if it's divided by walls, hills, and countless other things. The substance created things share is single, even if it's divided among countless bodies, each with its own individual properties. Soul is single, even if it's divided among countless natures and individual entities. Intelligent soul is single, even if it seems to be disunited.

# — ON —
# TRUTH

---

Any act of injustice is an impious act, because universal nature has made rational beings to help one another and benefit one another as they deserve, without ever doing harm, and to transgress against the will of universal nature is plainly to sin against the eldest of the gods and goddesses. Lying too is a sin against the same goddess, because universal nature is the nature of existing things, and existing things and the facts are intimately related. Universal nature is also called Truth, and is the original source of everything that is true. So anyone who lies intentionally is committing an impious act, insofar as he wrongs people by deceiving them; but anyone who lies unintentionally is also committing an impious act, insofar as he clashes with universal nature and wields disorder in a fight against the orderly universe. After all, anyone who resists truth is involved in a fight, and one of his own making, because he's been granted the necessary resources by nature, and it's his neglect of these resources that has made him incapable now of distinguishing falsehood from truth.

———

When the luminous sphere of the soul neither reaches out for anything external nor shrinks back inside itself, it suffers no inflation or collapse, and shines with a light that enables it to see the truth of all things and the truth within itself.

If someone can prove me wrong and show me that something I thought or did was mistaken, I'll gladly change, because my goal is the truth and the truth has never harmed anyone. The person who's harmed is the one who persists in his own self-deception and ignorance.

# — ON —
# VANITY

---

How rapidly everything vanishes, physical bodies lost in the universe and the memory of them
lost in eternity! Look at the nature of every object
we perceive, especially those that entice us with
the prospect of pleasure, frighten us with the
prospect of pain, or are celebrated by humans
in their vanity! How worthless, vile, sordid, and
short-lived things are, just corpses!

---

Vanity is terrifyingly good at derailing rational thought, and it's when you think you're engaged on important matters that you're most under its spell.

———

Continually remind yourself of all those highly dissatisfied men who pushed the boundaries of fortune in one way or another—in terms of fame, perhaps, or catastrophes met with, or enemies made. And then ask yourself: Where is it all now? Smoke and ashes, the stuff of stories or not even that. How worthless was all that expenditure of effort! How much more philosophical it is for someone to use the materials he's been given to make himself a man of justice and moderation, a follower of the gods—and to do so in an unaffected way, because there's no one more unbearable than a man who, in his delusion, boasts about his lack of vanity.

———

## — ON —
# THE VIRTUES

They can't admire you for perspicacity, but that's all right: there are many other qualities for which "I wasn't made that way" doesn't provide you with an excuse. The qualities you can offer, then, are those which are entirely up to you: candor, dignity, endurance, indifference to pleasure, acceptance of your lot, frugality, kindness, self-reliance, unaffectedness, discretion, stateliness. Do you see how many you're able to offer right now, without excusing yourself on the grounds of ineptitude and incompetence? And yet you persist, of your own free will, in doing worse than your best. Or is it innate ineptitude that compels you to grumble, to be stingy, to flatter, to blame your body, to be obsequious, to brag, to change your mind so often? No, most certainly not! You could have eliminated these faults a long time ago and been convicted, if at all, *only* of being rather slow and dull-witted. Yet even this can be worked on—as long as a person doesn't disregard or even relish his stupidity.

———

Good and bad for a rational and social being lie not in passivity but in action, just as virtue and vice for him lie not in passivity but in action.

———

This thing that is now causing an impression in my mind: What is it? What is it made of? How long will it last, given what it is? What virtue is called for in its case? Not that this is a complete list, but is it calmness, perhaps, or courage, honesty, fidelity, unaffectedness, self-sufficiency? In each case, then, here's what you must say: "This has come from God"; or "This is an accidental result of the web woven by fate and a fortuitous coincidence of some kind"; or "This has come from one of my own kind, someone who is kin and a member of the same society, but who's ignorant of what's in accord with his nature." But I *do* know, and so I treat him with kindness and justice, in accordance with the natural laws of human intercourse, but at the same time I aim for equity, dealing with him as he deserves, when it comes to things that are morally neutral.

When doing something, don't be sluggish; when talking to people, don't be muddled; when thinking, don't be vague. Don't ever let your soul contract or leap. Don't fill your life with busyness. "They kill you, butcher you, hound you with curses." But does this in any way stop you preserving the purity, lucidity, moderation, and justice of your mind? Suppose someone standing by a clear, sweet spring were to curse it: it just keeps right on bringing drinkable water bubbling up to the surface. Even if he throws mud or dung in it, before long the spring disperses the dirt and washes it out, leaving no stain. So how are you to have the equivalent of an ever-flowing spring? If you preserve your self-reliance at every hour, and your kindness, simplicity, and morality.

You know from personal experience that in all your detours the good life was nowhere to be found: not in logic, or wealth, or prestige, or sensual pleasure—nowhere. So where is it to be found? In doing what your human nature requires. And how is one to do this? By adhering to principles that guide your impulses and actions. What principles? Those that are concerned with good and bad, and state that nothing is good for a human being except what makes him honest, moderate, courageous, and self-reliant, and that nothing is bad except what inculcates the opposite qualities in him.

Never count something to your advantage if it's ever going to force you to break a promise, relinquish your modesty, hate or suspect or curse anyone, dissemble, or desire something that needs to be concealed behind walls or curtains.

———————

In applying your principles, you must be a pancratiast rather than a gladiator. A gladiator lays his sword aside and takes it up, but a pancratiast is never without his hands and all he has to do is make fists of them.

———————

You must get into the habit of restricting your thoughts to those which are such that if you were suddenly asked, "What are you thinking?," you could answer, frankly and without hesitation, "X" or "Y," and it would immediately be clear from your reply that all your thoughts are guileless and kindly, the thoughts of a sociable creature who disdains pleasurable or any kind of self-indulgent fantasies, and is untouched by rivalry, malice, suspicion, or anything else that one would blush to admit one had in mind.

Dig inside yourself. Inside you, there's a well-spring of goodness, which is capable of gushing all the time, as long as you keep digging.

# — ON —
# WORK

---

No form of toil is unnatural for the hand or the foot, as long as the foot is doing the work of a foot and the hand the work of a hand. By the same token, no form of toil is unnatural for a human being either, qua human being, as long as he's doing human work. And if it's not unnatural for him, it's not bad for him either.

---

---

Is my mind capable of dealing with this or not? If it is, I put it to work as an instrument granted me by universal nature. If it isn't, I either cede the work to someone who's better equipped to carry it out, or, if it's something that's not appropriate for another person, I do what I can, enlisting the help of someone who's able, by working with my command center, to do what's appropriate and good for the community at this moment in time. For whether I act on my own or with someone else's assistance, all my actions should be directed solely toward what is socially useful and fitting.

---

There's no shame in being helped, because you've got to do the job you've been set, like a soldier storming a city wall. Suppose you had a limp and were unable to scale the battlements on your own, but could do so with someone else's assistance.

Every time you do something, ask yourself: "Do I find this acceptable? Might I not come to regret it?"

---

Does the sun take on the work of the rain? Does Asclepius take on the work of the Lady of the Harvest? What about the heavenly bodies? Each of them is different, but they still work together toward the same end.

# —— ON ——
# THE WORLD

———

Take the time of Vespasian, for example, and you'll see the same old things: people marrying, raising a family, getting sick, dying, making war, celebrating festivals, trading, farming, flattering, acting in their own interests, being mistrustful, scheming, praying for their enemies to die, grumbling at their circumstances, falling in love, storing up wealth, longing for the consulship or sole rule. And now not a trace remains of that life of theirs. Then turn to the time of Trajan and it's the same all over again; that life too has died. Likewise, if you consider the histories of other periods and peoples in their entirety, you'll see how all those men sweated and toiled, and then died a short while later and were resolved into their elements.

———

Some things are rushing toward existence, others rushing to have done with existence, and in a certain respect anything that comes into existence is already extinguished. The world is continuously being renewed by flux and alteration, just as infinite time is forever being renewed by the uninterrupted flow of time. In this torrent of instability, which of the things that are flying past might one value? It's as if one were to begin to feel affection for a certain sparrow as it flew past—but it's already gone from sight.

———

Things are so veiled, as one might put it, that quite a few philosophers, and not the least eminent ones at that, claim that it's impossible for us to achieve the slightest degree of cognitive certainty about them, while even the Stoics regard things as hard to grasp with certainty. And then what about the actual objects of the world, which underlie our impressions? See how transient and worthless they are, and how they can belong to perverts, prostitutes, and thieves. And then what about your acquaintances, character-wise? See how even the most refined of them are hard to tolerate—not to mention how difficult it is to endure even oneself. Given all this gloom and grime, given the great flux of being and time, of movement and moving things, I cannot begin to comprehend what there is in it to value or take at all seriously.

Watch the stars in their courses as though you were accompanying them, and reflect constantly on the changing of the elements into one another. A mind that is impressed in these ways is cleansed of the filth of life on earth.

---

There's nothing here that isn't experientially familiar, temporally impermanent, and constitutionally squalid. Everything now is just as it was in the time of those we've buried.

---

# — ON —
# WRONGDOING

---

Remember that you yourself often do wrong and are no better than them. Even if you refrain from certain kinds of transgressions, you still have the *capacity* to commit them, and it's just cowardice or a concern for your reputation or some other equally bad reason that keeps you from committing the same kind of wrongs as them.

---

When you get the impression that someone has done wrong, ask yourself: "How can I actually know that it was a wrong?" And if it really was a wrong, remember that he was thereby passing sentence on himself, and that his wrongdoing was therefore the equivalent of poking himself in the eye. Remember that anyone who wants a bad man not to do wrong is like someone wanting a fig tree not to produce sap, or babies not to cry, or horses not to neigh, or anything else not to do what it's bound to do. I mean, if that's his disposition, what else can he do? So, if you feel strongly about it, change his disposition for the better.

Iniquity in general has no harmful effect on the universe, and individual iniquity harms not the person at the receiving end, but only the perpetrator, and he has the possibility of ridding himself of it. He only has to make that choice.

Wrongdoing isn't the outcome just of action, but often of inaction as well.

David Stuttard

**Robin Waterfield** is a British classical scholar, translator, and editor, specializing in ancient Greek philosophy and history. Among others, his translations include Plato's *Republic*, Herodotus's *The Histories*, and *Aesop's Fables*. He lives in Greece.